J BIO GRANT
Englar, Mary.
Union general and 18th president :
lysses S. Grant /

UNION GENERAL AND 18TH PRESIDENT
ULYSSES S. GRANT

by Mary Englar

Content Adviser:
Aaron Lisec, Associate Editor,
Papers of Ulysses S. Grant

Reading Adviser: Alexa L. Sandmann, Ed.D.,
Professor of Literacy, College and Graduate School
of Education, Health and Human Services,
Kent State University

Compass Point Books ✦ Minneapolis, Minnesota

Compass Point Books
151 Good Counsel Drive
P.O. Box 669
Mankato, MN 56002-0669

 This book was manufactured with paper containing at least 10 percent post-consumer waste.

On the cover: Ulysses S. Grant and his generals on horseback. Lithograph by E. Boell, c. 1865.

Photographs ©: Library of Congress, cover, 6, 7, 20, 25, 29, 38; North Wind Picture Archives, 5, 10, 11, 13, 34, 35, 36; Mary Evans Picture Library, 8; The Granger Collection, New York, 9, 17, 18, 21, 23, 27, 32; Line of Battle Enterprise, 15; Private Collection/The Bridgeman Art Library, 30; MPI/Getty Images, 33; Corbis, 39; ClassicStock/Alamy, 40; Philip Lange/iStockphoto, 41.

Editor: Sue Vander Hook
Page Production: Bobbie Nuytten
Photo Researcher: Svetlana Zhurkin
Cartographer: XNR Productions, Inc.
Library Consultant: Kathleen Baxter

Art Director: LuAnn Ascheman-Adams
Creative Director: Joe Ewest
Editorial Director: Nick Healy
Managing Editor: Catherine Neitge

Library of Congress Cataloging-in-Publication Data
Englar, Mary.
   Union general and 18th president : Ulysses S. Grant / by Mary Englar.
      p. cm. — (We the people)
Includes index.
   ISBN: 978-0-7565-4113-2 (library binding)
   1. Grant, Ulysses S. (Ulysses Simpson), 1822–1885—Juvenile literature. 2. Presidents—United States—Biography—Juvenile literature. 3. Generals—United States—Biography—Juvenile literature. 4. United States—Army—Biography—Juvenile literature. I. Title. II. Title: union general and eighteenth president.
E672.E65 2009
973.8'2092—dc22
[B]   2008037631

Visit Compass Point Books on the Internet at *www.compasspointbooks.com*
or e-mail your request to *custserv@compasspointbooks.com*

Table of Contents

"Let Us Have Peace" • 4

Growing Up in Ohio • 8

Searching for a Career • 15

The War Between the States • 22

President Grant • 31

Final Achievement • 37

Glossary • 42

Did You Know? • 43

Important Dates • 44

Important People • 45

Want to Know More? • 46

Index • 48

"Let Us Have Peace"

On the morning of March 4, 1869, Ulysses S. Grant dressed in his best black suit and a pair of yellow gloves. He looked at the cloudy sky from his bedroom window. A steady drizzle dampened the spirits of his excited family. Grant had experienced far worse weather during the American Civil War. A little rain would not spoil the most important day of his life.

Grant climbed into his carriage with his military assistant, John Rawlins, and drove to the U.S. Capitol. The streets were filled with Americans who had come to Washington, D.C., to see the famous general. All along Pennsylvania Avenue, people tried to catch a glimpse of General Grant, now the 18th president of the United States.

When Grant stepped onto the platform on the Capitol steps, the crowd cheered at the sight of him. Grant took the oath of office and stepped forward to read his inaugural address. He told his audience that the Civil War had created new problems for the government. In order for the United States to remain strong, its citizens must solve the problems "without prejudice, hate, or

*Ulysses S. Grant,
18th president of the United States*

sectional pride, remembering that the greatest good to the greatest number is the object to be attained."

After the speech, Grant and his family attended the inaugural parade. Thousands of U.S. soldiers marched down the street to honor the new president. Later that evening, the Grants

The crowd focused its attention on President Ulysses S. Grant and his wife, Julia, when they arrived at the inaugural ball in Washington, D.C.

danced at the inaugural ball held at the new Treasury Building. With his wife, Julia, by his side, Grant greeted and bowed to hundreds of admiring guests. At midnight, his family finally sat down to supper.

Until the Civil War broke out, Grant had barely been able to support his family. But he was quite successful in the Union Army, rising quickly in rank and motivating his men to fight hard. His victory over Confederate General Robert E. Lee brought an end to the bloodiest war ever fought in the United States. Many Americans believed that Grant's military skill was the reason the North had won the war.

Grant hated the bloody battles and the loss of so many young soldiers, but he strongly believed that the United States must remain united. When the Republican Party nominated him to run for president in 1868, his acceptance letter ended with these words: "Let us have peace." It would take all his skill to unite Americans once again.

"Let Us Have Peace," a poem written in 1868, was illustrated with events in Grant's life.

Growing Up in Ohio

Hiram Ulysses Grant was born April 27, 1822, in Point Pleasant, Ohio. His parents, Jesse and Hannah Grant, had no idea what to name their first child. They asked their relatives to help them choose a name for their new baby boy.

Birthplace of Ulysses S. Grant in Point Pleasant, Ohio

Each relative put a favorite name into a hat. Jesse pulled out the name Ulysses and shook his head. Then he drew out another name—Hiram. This was the name he wanted for his son. Hannah and her mother thought Ulysses should be his name since it was the first one drawn out of the hat. In the end, the baby was named Hiram Ulysses Grant. His parents called him Ulysses.

About a year later, the Grants moved to Georgetown, Ohio. It was a new town with only 15 houses. Jesse had learned the hide tanning business as a young man, so he opened a local

*Hannah Simpson Grant and
Jesse Root Grant*

9

In the 1800s, tanners used knives to scrape hair from animal hides and make them into leather used for shoes and clothes.

tannery. Jesse's business did well. He scraped animal hides and tanned them into leather.

Across the street from the tannery, Jesse built a small brick home. There his family would grow to six children—three boys and three girls. Education was important to Jesse. He sent all his children to a one-room school in town. Because there were no free schools nearby, Jesse had to pay tuition for each of his children.

Ulysses found school very boring. His school had 30 to 40 students of all ages, and there was one teacher—Mr. White—who taught every subject, from the alphabet to math. White often whipped the children with branches to make them behave.

Young students learned to speak in front of the class in 19th-century schools.

Ulysses was whipped, too, but he still remembered his teacher as a kind man.

When he wasn't in school, Ulysses helped his father with chores. He hated the tannery. It smelled terrible, and the sight of blood made Ulysses sick. He preferred to take care of their farm animals and plant crops. By the time he was 11, Ulysses was plowing, planting, and harvesting corn and potato crops. He also chopped wood and hauled it from the woods to the house.

Ulysses was fascinated with the family horses. He liked any work that included riding, driving, or plowing. He even helped his neighbors tame their young horses. Ulysses could ride any horse, even the wild ones. His respect and love for the animal would stay with him all his life.

Though Jesse expected Ulysses to work hard, he also gave him freedom to choose his activities. Ulysses fished and swam in the summer and ice-skated in the winter. He often drove a horse

A farm boy helped in the fields by leading a team of horses while his father plowed.

and sleigh to visit his grandparents who lived 15 miles (24 kilo-

meters) away. Ulysses didn't ask for much from his parents. He

was a quiet, serious child.

As Ulysses got older, Jesse wondered what his oldest son

would do with his life. Ulysses didn't like to study, although he did enjoy reading and excelled at math. But most of all, he hated the tannery.

Jesse heard about an opening at the U.S. Military Academy at West Point, New York. He thought it might give Ulysses good preparation for a career as an engineer or an officer in the Army. Jesse sent Ulysses to a boarding school to prepare him for the academy and requested an appointment.

Before long, Ulysses received an appointment to the academy from Congressman Thomas Hamer. But Hamer made a mistake on the application. He thought Jesse's son was named Ulysses. He didn't know that his first name was Hiram. When he needed to fill in a middle name, he put S for Simpson, the last name of Ulysses' mother before she married Jesse Grant. From then on, Hiram Ulysses Grant was known as Ulysses S. Grant.

3 Searching for a Career

hen Ulysses S. Grant arrived at West Point in 1839, military rules proved difficult. He didn't have a good sense of rhythm and found it hard to march in time with the other cadets.

The U.S. Military Acadamy at West Point was situated on high ground above a narrow curve in the Hudson River.

Grant managed to pass his classes, but he didn't see a future in the military.

Grant enjoyed reading and checked out many books from the library. But his favorite times were spent in horsemanship. He handled the most challenging horses easily. In his senior year, he set a record for jumping. He thought he might like the cavalry after he graduated.

When Grant graduated from West Point in 1843, his grades placed him 21st out of 39 students. With average grades, Grant didn't get his choice of the cavalry. Although he was the best horseman in his class, he was assigned to the infantry—foot soldiers. Grant, now a second lieutenant, joined his unit near St. Louis, Missouri.

Grant's good friend at West Point, Frederick Dent, was from St. Louis. Dent suggested that Grant visit the Dent family when he had free time. Grant followed his friend's advice and went to see Dent's family. He played with the younger children and often joined the family for dinner. Their oldest daughter was 17-year-old Julia, with whom Grant quickly fell in love. She was energetic and had beautiful eyes. And, like Grant, she enjoyed horses and was a good rider.

In 1845, Grant's unit was ordered to Louisiana. But before he left, he secretly proposed to Julia. She accepted and agreed to marry him when he came back. That fall, Grant was sent to Texas, where the United States was about to go to war with Mexico over land disputes.

Julia Dent was raised at White Haven plantation near St. Louis, Missouri.

Ulysses S. Grant was a second lieutenant in the Mexican War.

In his job as quarter-master, Grant bought supplies for his unit and packed mules and wagons with food, clothing, and ammunition. Grant's job was important, but he wanted to prove himself in battle. When he got his chance, he impressed his fellow soldiers with his bravery and ability to make good decisions.

After the war, Grant hurried back to Julia. They told their parents they wanted to get married, but neither side was happy about it. Julia's father believed Grant had little ambition. Grant's father didn't want his son marrying into a family who owned slaves. But Grant and Julia were in love and got married

August 22, 1848, at Julia's home. They were happy together, even though they had to move often whenever Grant received new assignments. After several months in New York, he was sent to Detroit, Michigan.

On May 30, 1850, the young couple welcomed their first child—Frederick, named after Julia's father. Two years later, in 1852, Grant's unit was ordered to Fort Vancouver in Oregon. Grant knew he couldn't take Julia and his young son on such a long, dangerous journey. Besides, Julia was now expecting their second child. So Julia and young Frederick returned to live with her family, and Grant left for Oregon.

Grant loved being a husband and father. He missed his family constantly and waited eagerly for each letter from Julia. Letters traveled thousands of miles by ship and took months to arrive. As time passed, Grant grew so unhappy and lonely that he resigned from the Army in 1854.

Ulysses S. Grant with his wife, Julia, and their four children

When Grant returned to St. Louis, he saw his second son, Ulysses, for the first time. The toddler, nicknamed Buck, was now 2 years old. Grant built a house and planted crops on land his father-in-law gave him. When his first crops didn't make money, he sold firewood for extra income. Grant's family was growing. In 1855, they had a daughter, Ellen, nicknamed Nellie. Three years later, they welcomed another son, Jesse. Although Grant worked very hard, he couldn't earn enough money to support his family.

In 1860, Grant moved his family to Galena, Illinois. There he worked in his father's leather goods store. Grant's brothers managed the business, and Grant worked as a clerk. Although he didn't earn much money, it was enough to support his growing family.

Grant worked at his father's leather goods store in Galena, Illinois, for two years.

4 The War Between the States

While Ulysses S. Grant was quietly working in Illinois, a disagreement between the states in the North and the South was heating up. They had very different views on the issue of slavery. They also disagreed on whether the federal government should make decisions for individual states. It was an election year in 1860. Some Southern states threatened to secede if Abraham Lincoln was elected. They feared he would abolish slavery.

After Lincoln was elected, 11 Southern states did indeed secede from the United States. They set up their own government, a new country called the Confederate States of America. They approved a constitution and named Jefferson Davis their new president. President Lincoln warned the South not to attack Union military forts located in the South. Even so, on April 12, 1861, Confederate forces fired on Fort Sumter in South Carolina.

Grant immediately volunteered to help raise an army in Galena, Illinois, to support the Northern cause. Congressman Elihu Washburne recommended that Grant take charge of the 21st Illinois Regiment. What Grant found was a group of

In 1861, Grant left his family and home in Galena, Illinois, to serve in the Union Army.

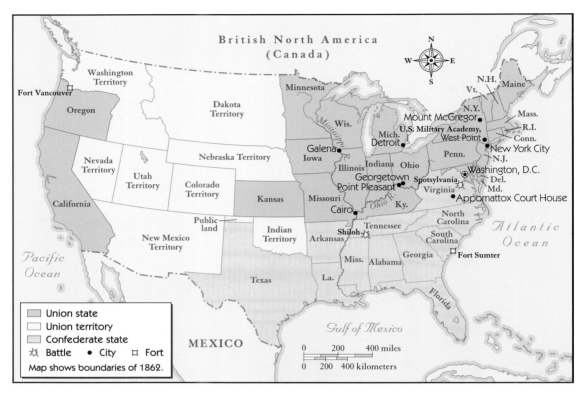

Grant lived much of his life in Ohio and Illinois, but his military career took him to places such as New York, Oregon, and several Southern states.

volunteers, mostly farmers, who lacked training and discipline. But he soon got them ready for war.

Grant's first big assignment was to protect the important junction of the Ohio and Mississippi rivers at Cairo, Illinois. His unit protected the North from invasion by the Confederate Army along the Mississippi. Grant wanted to take action, not wait for the battle to come to him. Using gunboats to protect his soldiers, he led his men into battle against two Southern forts that protected the Tennessee River.

His men took Fort Henry easily, but Fort Donelson was more difficult. The Confederate soldiers fought hard and destroyed Grant's gunboats. Grant surrounded the fort and cut

Grant demanded that the Confederate Army surrender unconditionally at the Battle of Fort Donelson. His victory earned him the nickname "Unconditional Surrender" Grant.

off their escape. Two days later, about 15,000 Confederate soldiers surrendered to Grant. When Lincoln heard of Grant's success, he promoted him to major general of volunteers.

Not all of Grant's battles went well. At Shiloh, Tennessee, the Confederate Army launched a surprise attack on the Union camp. Grant was 9 miles (14.5 km) away. He jumped into a boat, shouting orders for his men to march to Shiloh. At Shiloh, Grant's men faced 62 Confederate cannons. As quickly as they pressed forward, the cannons cut them down.

Grant expected reinforcements to join him, but they took another day to arrive. When they got there, Grant ordered the combined forces to push the Confederates back. They were successful, but the Union Army lost about 13,000 men. The Confederates lost 10,700. It was the largest and bloodiest battle of the war up to that time.

During the winter of 1862 to 1863, Grant's soldiers

approached Vicksburg, Mississippi, where Confederate troops

controlled the Mississippi River. By the summer, after months of

fighting, Grant surrounded the city, capturing it on July 4, 1863.

President Lincoln watched Grant's growing accomplish-

ments. In March 1864, he promoted Grant to lieutenant general

After nearly three weeks of fighting, Union troops trapped Confederate soldiers in the city of Vicksburg, Mississippi.

and put him in charge of the entire Union Army. For three years, the Union Army had been unable to defeat Confederate General Robert E. Lee. Lincoln and Grant agreed that Lee had to be defeated if the Union was to win the war.

Grant moved his 127,000 soldiers into Virginia. Lee, an experienced soldier, forced Grant into many bloody battles there. After the five-day battle at Spotsylvania, Grant lost 18,000 men. He wrote to Julia about the loss of his soldiers: "The world has never seen so bloody and so protracted a battle as the one being fought and I hope never will again."

Despite his losses, Grant forced Lee south until he surrounded him at Richmond, Virginia, the Confederate capital. From June 1864 until April 1865, the two generals held their positions. Both sides planned attacks from time to time, but finally the Confederate soldiers lost strength. Lee's men were starving and needed ammunition and clothing.

The Battle of Spotsylvania was fought where the Rapidan and Rappahannock rivers meet in central Virginia.

Grant sent a message to Lee asking him to talk about terms of surrender. They agreed to meet on April 9, 1865, at the home of Wilmer McLean in the town of Appomattox Court House, Virginia. There the two men discussed surrender. Grant asked the Confederate soldiers to turn over their arms. Then he would let them return home. Lee asked Grant to allow his men to

Confederate General Robert E. Lee (center) surrendered to Union General Ulysses S. Grant on April 9, 1865, bringing an end to the Civil War.

keep their horses and mules. Grant agreed, and Lee accepted the

terms of surrender. After nearly four years, the bloodiest war in

U.S. history was over.

On April 14, 1865, Grant met with Lincoln and his Cabinet.

That evening, Lincoln invited Grant and Julia to join him at the

theater, but the Grants wanted to see their children. President

Lincoln was assassinated that night by John Wilkes Booth.

President Grant

After the war, Ulysses S. Grant was a national hero. On July 25, 1866, Congress created a new military position. Grant was named general of the armies of the United States. It was the highest rank ever given to an American soldier. Everywhere Grant went, people offered him gifts. He received money, several houses, and 14 horses.

Grant's popularity grew, and in 1868, he was elected president of the United States. Four years later he would be elected again for a second term. The man who had once been an average student and wondered what he would do with his life was now the president. He held the highest position in the land.

At first, President Grant was highly admired. After all, he had won the war and was an American hero. Most Americans expected him to be a good president. However, Grant was not prepared for the problems he faced.

Grant had never been a good businessman, and he found running the government difficult. He gave important positions to his friends and family members. Though he trusted them to make

Many of Grant's Cabinet members were inexperienced, which weakened Grant's presidency.

good decisions, some of them were dishonest. Grant was blamed for their actions, and he lost his heroic image with some people. However, most Americans still respected this great hero of the Civil War.

The war had

A cartoon depicted Grant burdened by the problems he faced as president and pursued by the press (hounds).

left all Americans deeply divided. One of Grant's biggest jobs was to protect former slaves. He had to figure out how to make citizens out of slaves freed by the war. He pushed for an amendment to the U.S. Constitution that would guarantee all races the right to vote.

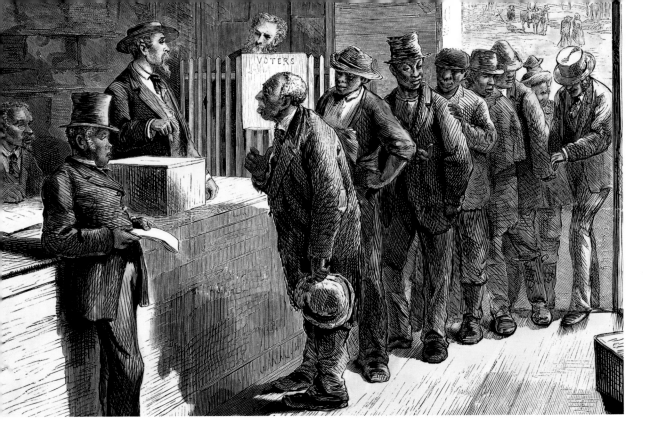

The 15th Amendment gave African-American men the right to vote.

The 15th Amendment was passed in 1870, but armed groups in some Southern states prevented black citizens from voting. Grant had to send soldiers to help protect their rights.

Grant also tried to solve the problems between the Indians and settlers moving West. As America grew, the number of people moving to Western states was increasing. American settlers often ignored the Indian tribes' rights to their own lands.

Grant believed the Indians would be safer if they lived on reservations and learned to farm. He sent soldiers to force the Indians onto reservations. Many tribes fought both the soldiers and the settlers. Though Grant believed he was helping, the Indians lost huge amounts of land. Most of the reservation lands

Armed conflicts were common between the U.S. Army and Plains Indians.

Native Americans were forced to pack up their belongings and head to reservations, sometimes in the middle of winter.

they got in return were dry and not fit for farming. Many Indians became dependent on the government for their needs.

By the end of his second term, Grant was ready to leave government service. Although he and Julia loved Washington, D.C., and life at the White House, he decided not to run again for president in 1876.

In 1877, Grant boarded a steamship to Europe with Julia and their youngest son, Jesse. They had such a good time that they spent the next two years traveling around the world.

Final Achievement

The Grants returned from their worldwide trip in 1879. The nation proudly welcomed Ulysses S. Grant home as a hero once more. The Republican Party tried to nominate him for president in 1880, but no president had ever served a third term, and too many people opposed the idea.

Grant looked for ways to earn money. He traveled to the Rocky Mountains to inspect silver mines. He also went to Cuba and Mexico, where he tried to start a new railroad. Finally, Grant and Julia settled in New York City. Their son Ulysses was going into business with Ferdinand Ward, and Grant joined them, investing $100,000 in the stock market.

At first, the business seemed to do well. But in 1884, Grant discovered that Ward had cheated everyone. Ward stole what little money was left and disappeared.

Many of Grant's relatives and friends had also invested their money in this failed venture. Now Grant had to sell what he could to pay bills. Meanwhile, he accepted an offer to write four magazine articles about the Civil War. Grant discovered that he enjoyed writing.

Mark Twain (Samuel Langhorne Clemens)
(1835–1910)

When his articles were published, author Mark Twain asked to see him. He offered Grant a contract to write the story of his life.

Not long after he began to write his book, Grant noticed a pain in his throat when he swallowed. His doctor told him it was incurable cancer. Now Grant worried about how Julia would survive after he was gone.

Despite terrible suffering, Grant threw himself into writing his book. If he could finish it, the money from the sales would take care of Julia and his family after he died. Grant's throat got

When Grant was ill with cancer, he spent most of his time reading and writing his memoirs.

Near the end of his life, Grant (seated with top hat) posed for a family picture on the porch of his Mount McGregor home in New York.

so bad that he lost his speech and had to write little notes to his family. But in spite of his poor health, he kept writing.

In the summer of 1885, the Grants moved to Mount McGregor, where Grant finished his book in June. On July 23, 1885, Ulysses S. Grant died. He was 63. A train transported his body to New York City, where thousands of people lined the tracks in a funeral parade that stretched 7 miles (11 km), Americans still considered him a hero. Their beloved general and president was buried in New York City at Riverside Park by the Hudson River. His tomb bears his words, "Let us have peace."

Grant's tomb in New York City, a national monument and the largest tomb in North America, is a memorial to Grant's life and accomplishments.

Glossary

assassinate—to murder an important person, such as a president

cadet—person training to become a member of the armed forces

cavalry—soldiers who ride horses

Confederacy—the Southern states that broke away from the federal government and fought against the Northern states in the Civil War; also called the Confederate States of America

inaugural—referring to a formal induction into office, especially the presidency

infantry—soldiers who fight on foot

secede—to formally withdraw from an organization, state, or country

tannery—place where animal skins are scraped, soaked, and changed into leather

Union—the Northern states that fought against the Southern states in the Civil War

Did You Know?

- More than 3 million Americans fought in the Civil War; more than 620,000 men died from battle wounds and disease.

- The city of Vicksburg was under siege for 38 days. On July 4, 1863, Confederate General John C. Pemberton surrendered the city to Major General Ulysses S. Grant; for the next 81 years, the Fourth of July was not celebrated in Vicksburg.

- Grant is featured on the $50 bill.

- In 1872, Grant signed a bill to create the first national park at Yellowstone.

- Grant's daughter Nellie got married in the White House in 1874.

- After his presidency, Grant became president of the Mexican Southern Railroad Company; he encouraged trade between Mexico and the United States and negotiated a trade agreement with Mexico in 1883, though Congress failed to approve it.

Important Dates

Timeline

1822	Born April 27 in Point Pleasant, Ohio
1843	Graduates from the U.S. Military Academy at West Point, New York
1845	Goes to Texas with the 4th U.S. Infantry to fight in the Mexican War
1848	Marries Julia Dent August 22 in St. Louis, Missouri
1850	First child, Frederick Dent Grant, is born
1861	Joins the Union Army at the start of the Civil War
1862	Leads attacks on Fort Henry and Fort Donelson, followed by the Battle of Shiloh
1863	Captures Vicksburg on July 4, after months of marching and fighting
1864	Commands entire Union Army
1865	Accepts Confederate surrender on April 9 at Appomattox Court House
1868	Elected president of the United States; serves two terms
1877	Takes two-year trip around the world with wife, Julia, and son Jesse
1885	Dies July 23 of throat cancer in Mount McGregor, New York

Important People

Samuel Clemens (1835–1910)
Author and publisher known by his pen name, Mark Twain, read Grant's magazine articles about the war and offered him a contract to write his life story; Personal Memoirs of U.S. Grant, *published after Grant's death, sold well; the proceeds paid his family nearly half a million dollars*

Robert E. Lee (1807–1870)
Confederate general who led the Army of Northern Virginia during the Civil War; after the war, he became president of Washington College in Lexington, Virginia; when he died, he was buried in the chapel; today the school is named Washington and Lee University

Abraham Lincoln (1809–1865)
The 16th president of the United States from 1861 to 1865; believed that the country must be united, even if it meant a war between the North and the South; issued the Emancipation Proclamation in 1863 to free all slaves in the Confederate states; became the first American president to be assassinated when John Wilkes Booth shot him on April 14, 1865; he died the next day

John A. Rawlins (1831–1869)
Headed Grant's staff during the Civil War; he was Grant's most trusted adviser and good friend; after the war, Grant named him secretary of war, but he only served for five months before he died

Want to Know More?

More Books to Read

Aller, Susan Bivin. *Ulysses S. Grant.* Minneapolis: Lerner Publications Co., 2005.

Murray, Aaron R., ed. *Civil War: Battles and Leaders.* New York: DK Publishing, 2004.

Rice, Earle Jr. *Ulysses S. Grant: Defender of the Union.* Greensboro, N.C.: Morgan Reynolds Publishing, 2005.

Santella, Andrew. *Surrender at Appomattox.* Minneapolis: Compass Point Books, 2006.

Sapp, Richard. *Ulysses S. Grant and the Road to Appomattox.* Milwaukee: World Almanac Library, 2006.

On the Web

For more information on this topic, use FactHound.

1. Go to *www.facthound.com*

2. Choose your grade level.

3. Begin your search.

This book's ID number is 9780756541132

FactHound will find the best sites for you.

On the Road

General Grant National Memorial
122nd Street and Riverside Drive
New York, NY 10027
212/666-1640
Burial site of Grant and his wife, Julia Dent Grant

Ulysses S. Grant National Historic Site
7400 Grant Road
St. Louis, MO 63123
314/842-1867
White Haven, the house where Julia Dent Grant grew up and where Grant and Julia once lived; the site honors Grant's life, military career, and political career

Look for more We the People Biographies:

American Patriot: Benjamin Franklin
Civil War Spy: Elizabeth Van Lew
Confederate Commander: General Robert E. Lee
Confederate General: Stonewall Jackson
First of First Ladies: Martha Washington
A Signer for Independence: John Hancock
Soldier and Founder: Alexander Hamilton

A complete list of We the People titles is available on our Web site:
www.compasspointbooks.com

Index

15th Amendment, 34
21st Illinois Regiment, 23–24

American Civil War, 5, 6–7, 22–30, 33, 38

Battle of Shiloh, 26
Battle of Spotsylvania, 28
Battle of Vicksburg, 27
birth, 8
Booth, John Wilkes, 30

childhood, 9, 12–13
Civil War. *See* American Civil War.
Confederate Army, 6–7, 22, 24, 25, 26, 27, 28, 29
Confederate States of America, 22

Davis, Jefferson, 22
death, 40–41
Dent, Frederick, 16–17

education, 10–12, 14

Fort Donelson, 25–26
Fort Henry, 25
Fort Sumter, 22
Fort Vancouver, 19

grandparents, 13

Grant, Ellen (daughter), 21, 30
Grant, Frederick (son), 19, 30
Grant, Hannah (mother), 8, 9, 14
Grant, Jesse (father), 8, 9–10, 12, 13–14, 18, 21
Grant, Jesse (son), 21, 30, 36
Grant, Julia (wife), 6, 17, 18–19, 28, 30, 36, 37, 39
Grant, Ulysses "Buck" (son), 20, 30, 37

Hamer, Thomas, 14
health, 38–39, 39–40
horsemanship, 12, 16, 17, 31

inauguration, 4–6
Indians, 34–36
investments, 37–38

Lee, Robert E., 6–7, 28, 29–30
Lincoln, Abraham, 22, 26, 27–28, 30

map, 24
marriage, 18–19
McLean, Wilmer, 29
Mexican War, 17–18
military service, 4, 6–7, 14, 15–16, 17–18, 19, 23–26, 26–30

name, 9, 14

presidency, 4–6, 31–33, 34, 35, 36, 37

Rawlins, John, 4
Republican Party, 7, 37
reservations, 35–36

secession, 22
settlers, 34, 35
siblings, 10, 21
slavery, 18, 22, 33

Twain, Mark, 38

Union Army, 6–7, 22, 26, 28
U.S. Congress, 14, 23, 31
U.S. Constitution, 33–34
U.S. Military Academy, 14, 15–16

voting rights, 33–34

Ward, Ferdinand, 37
Washburne, Elihu, 23
wealth, 37–38
writings, 38, 39, 40

About the Author

Mary Englar is a freelance writer and a teacher of English and creative writing. She has a master of fine arts degree in writing from Minnesota State University and has written more than 30 nonfiction books for children. She continues to read and write about history in Minnesota.